# THE STORY BEHIND

# WATER

Christin Ditchfield

Raintree

**www.raintreepublishers.co.uk**
Visit our website to find out more information about Raintree books.

**To order:**
☎ Phone 0845 6044371
🖹 Fax +44 (0) 1865 312263
🖳 Email myorders@raintreepublishers.co.uk

Customers from outside the UK please telephone +44 1865 312262

Raintree is an imprint of Capstone Global Library Limited, a company incorporated in England and Wales having its registered office at 7 Pilgrim Street, London, EC4V 6LB – Registered company number: 6695582

Edited by Megan Cotugno and Diyan Leake
Designed by Philippa Jenkins
Original illustrations © Capstone Global
    Library Ltd (2012)
Illustrated by Philippa Jenkins
Picture research by Hannah Taylor and Mica Brancic
Originated by Capstone Global Library Ltd
Printed and bound in China by CTPS

ISBN 978 1 406 22925 7 (hardback)
15 14 13 12 11
10 9 8 7 6 5 4 3 2 1

ISBN 978 1 406 22939 4 (paperback)
16 15 14 13 12
10 9 8 7 6 5 4 3 2 1

**British Library Cataloguing in Publication Data**
Ditchfield, Christin.
The story behind water. – (True stories)
553.7-dc22
A full catalogue record for this book is available from the British Library.

**Acknowledgements**
We would like to thank the following for permission to reproduce photographs: iStockphoto p. 27 (© Ivan Bajic); Shutterstock pp. iii (© Callahan ), 4 (© Alexander A. Trofimov), 5 (© April Cat), 6 (© Idreamphoto), 7 (© Jcreation), 8 (© Imagine Images/ Alastair Pidgen), 9 (© Anyunov), 10 (© Aaron Amat), 11 (© Ursula I Abresch), 12 (© Volodymyr Goinyk), 13 (© Jeff Martinez), 15 (© David Hughes ), 16 (© eAlisa), 17 (© Silver30), 18 (© Xavier Marchant), 20 (© Trevor Kittelty), 21 (© Wim Claes), 22 (© Zastol`skiy Victor Leonidovich), 23 (© Evok20), 24 (© Alex Balako), 25 (© Boris Khamitsevich), 26 (© Hector Conesa).

Cover photograph of drops falling down in water reproduced with permission of Alamy (© Nikola Bilic).

We would like to thank Ann Fullick for her invaluable help in the preparation of this book.

Every effort has been made to contact copyright holders of material reproduced in this book. Any omissions will be rectified in subsequent printings if notice is given to the publisher.

# Contents

Some words are shown in bold, **like this**.
You can find out what they mean by
looking in the glossary on page 30.

# Water, water everywhere!

 **In a waterfall, rushing water flows over a steep cliff.**

## Water world

Water covers 70 per cent of Earth's surface. All living things need water to survive. Without it, the living world could not exist.

Water is all around us. It is a **liquid** that pours down from rain clouds in the sky and splashes into the sea. It bubbles up in springs and flows in rivers. Trees and plants use their roots to soak up water from the ground. Water makes fruits and vegetables grow.

Everything we eat or drink has water in it. Although we can't see it, water is in the air we breathe. Human beings need fresh, clean water to drink. People also use water for washing and cooking.

# We are made of water

Plants, animals, and people are mostly made of water. In fact, water makes up between 60 and 70 per cent of a person's body weight. Water is in our brains, our lungs, our muscles, our bones, and our blood. Everything our bodies do requires water in some way.

## Are you thirsty?

We lose water from our bodies whenever we breathe or sweat or go to the toilet. It's important to replace it by drinking plenty of water each day. A person might be able to live for a month without food – but no one can live for much more than a week without water!

▼ To stay healthy, you need to have about 2.5 litres of water a day. You get this from food sources as well as drinks.

 A green sea turtle swims in the Caribbean Sea.

## A place to live

Thousands of creatures make their home in water. The ocean is full of different kinds of fish, otters, sea turtles, dolphins, and sharks. Ducks, beavers, and frogs live in ponds. Land animals drink water from nearby lakes, rivers, and creeks.

### On the job

A marine biologist is a scientist who studies all the plants and animals that live in the ocean. An oceanographer is a scientist who studies the ocean itself. Some oceanographers measure the waves and the **tides.** They chart the depths of the water. Some study how the ocean affects our weather. Others look for ways to protect the ocean from **pollution.**

## A place to work and play

For fishermen, sailors, and scientists, water is a place to work. For others, water is a place to play. People splash and swim and float in the cool, refreshing water. Athletes compete in water sports such as swimming, diving, canoeing, and water-skiing.

## A way to travel

For thousands of years, water has been one of the best ways to travel. Barges (large, flat-bottomed boats) carry large amounts of food, fuel, supplies, and equipment from one place to another. People sail on boats or ships. They travel through cities in waterways called canals.  Sometimes it's the only way to get from one place to another.

▼ People travel from place to place by boat in this water village in Shanghai, China.

▲ The Nile is the longest river in the world. It is about 6,700 kilometres (4,200 miles) long.

## Yesterday and today

The ancient Egyptians lived in a region of Africa where very little rain falls. They depended on the River Nile to water their crops. They used nets to catch fish and waterbirds. They took the reeds that grew by the river and turned them into paper and cloth. The Egyptians also used the river to travel from place to place and trade with other countries.

Between AD 100 and 200, the Romans created **aqueducts** – a system of bridges and tunnels – to carry large amounts of clean, fresh water throughout their cities. The water supplied wells, pools, and fountains.

Today, water generates electricity for homes, schools, farms, factories, and businesses. This **hydroelectricity** is one of the cleanest, most dependable, and least expensive sources of energy.

### Hippocrates (460–375 BC)

Hippocrates was a Greek doctor known as the "Father of Medicine". Long before anyone knew that water could carry **germs** and diseases, he told people that they should boil their water and strain it before drinking it. This killed the germs and made the water safe to drink.

▼ About 20 per cent of the world's electricity is generated by water power. China creates more hydroelectricity than any other country.

# What is water?

▶ The chemical formula for water is $H_2O$.

**Word power** ✔

Any word that starts with "hydro" or "hydra" – such as *hydroelectricity* – has something to do with water.

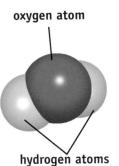

oxygen atom

hydrogen atoms

▲ This is a diagram of a water molecule.

Water is a **liquid** that is made up of two ingredients – hydrogen and oxygen. Two hydrogen **atoms** are joined to one oxygen atom to form a water **molecule**. This special liquid has no colour, taste, or smell. Water – like all liquids – takes the shape of whatever container it is placed in.

Water is known as a universal **solvent**, because it can dissolve or break down so many other substances. For instance, substances such as salt or sugar seem to disappear in water. You can taste them in the water, but you can't see them. They no longer have the same shape or texture that they did before. Water has many other qualities that make it unique.

## Not quite everything

There are a few substances that don't dissolve in water, such oils. They float on the surface of water instead. This is because oil molecules are attracted to other oil molecules – they stick together. Water molecules are attracted to other water molecules – they also stick together. The two just don't mix!

▼ **Drops of oil float on the surface of water.**

# Forms of water

▲ In the Southern Ocean around Antarctica, you can see water as a solid and as a liquid.

Water can be found naturally in three different forms: **liquid**, **solid**, and **gas**. Liquid water fills our lakes, rivers, and oceans. It comes out of a water fountain, a tap, or a hose. It can be splashed or sprayed.

When liquid water gets very cold, it freezes. Frozen water is hard and solid. We call it ice. It has a shape and takes up more space than water. Ice is not as heavy as liquid water, so it floats. When it floats, it insulates the water underneath it, forming a barrier between cold air and the water. This allows living things to survive in water over winter. If ice did not float, it would sink to the bottom and make the rest of the water too cold for most living things.

Sometimes water **evaporates**. Heat turns the liquid water into a gas. The gas – called **water vapour** – rises into the air.

Most of the time, water vapour is invisible. The steam that comes from your kettle is made of tiny drops of water. The water vapour turns back into a liquid as it cools down. This is called condensation. The same thing happens when clouds form in the sky. Water vapour in the air condenses in the cold and forms the tiny drops we see as mist or clouds.

▼ **These bison are outside on a cold day. The water vapour in their breath is condensing as they breathe out.**

fresh water 3%

salt water 97%

▶ **This pie chart shows how most of the water on Earth is salt water, not fresh water.**

## Salt water

The water in all oceans and some rivers is called salt water. The salt comes from rocks and **minerals** on the riverbed or the ocean floor. Some kinds of plants and animals can only live in salt water. However, this water is much too salty for people to drink.

**What's in a name?**

The Dead Sea in Israel is more than 30 per cent salt. This is nine times saltier than the ocean! It's so salty that only two kinds of **bacteria** (tiny living things) can live in it. There are no plants, fish, or marine animals at

# Fresh water

Fresh water can be found in rivers, lakes, and streams. It can also be found in wetlands – areas of standing water such as **swamps**, **marshes**, and **bogs**. Fresh water does not have the same salt and minerals that are found in ocean water. In fact, the salt content is less than 1 per cent. Different types of plants and animals live in fresh water. Fresh water is the water we use for drinking, washing, and cooking.

### A drop in the ocean ✔

Almost 97 per cent of the world's water is undrinkable. It may be too salty. About 2 per cent is frozen in **polar ice caps** and **glaciers**. Only 1 per cent can be used by human beings in their daily lives.

▼ A reservoir is an artificial lake created to store fresh water for future use.

# The water cycle

▲ Water evaporates from the surface of lakes, rivers, and oceans.

Although there is very little fresh water in the world, our supply has never run out. That's because water constantly **recycles** itself! Scientists call nature's recycling process the water cycle. In the water cycle, water moves from the earth up to the sky – and from the sky back down to the earth. This cycle is never-ending.

The sun heats up the water in rivers, lakes, and oceans. Some of the water **evaporates** and turns into **water vapour**, leaving any salt behind in the riverbed or on the ocean floor. The water vapour begins to rise from the surface of the earth. The wind blows it high into the sky.

As the water vapour rises higher, it starts to cool off and condense. Cold water vapour turns back into tiny drops of water. These little droplets stick together to form clouds. As more droplets join the clouds, the clouds get heavier and heavier.

### Way back when ✔

The water we drink has been drunk hundreds of times before by different people over thousands of years.

### Plants play a part ✔

Water is pulled up from the earth through the roots of plants. The plants lose the water through their leaves. This is called transpiration.

▼ Tiny droplets of water stick together to form clouds.

## The cycle continues

Soon the water begins to fall from the clouds as raindrops. (In very cold temperatures, the water freezes and turns to snow or **hail**.) Some of the rain sinks deep into the ground. It becomes part of the ground water that plants and animals drink. Some runs over the soil and collects in lakes and ponds. Some falls into rivers.

The rain that falls into the rivers will be slowly carried back to the ocean. There, the sun heats it up – and the whole cycle starts all over again. Water is always on the move.

▼ **Rain that falls in the mountains may form rivers that flow to the ocean.**

**What's in a name?**

The study of Earth's atmosphere, climate, and weather is called meteorology.

*Precipitation* is the word that describes any form of water that falls from the sky – rain, snow, or hail.

▼ **The water cycle is the way that Earth's water constantly recycles itself.**

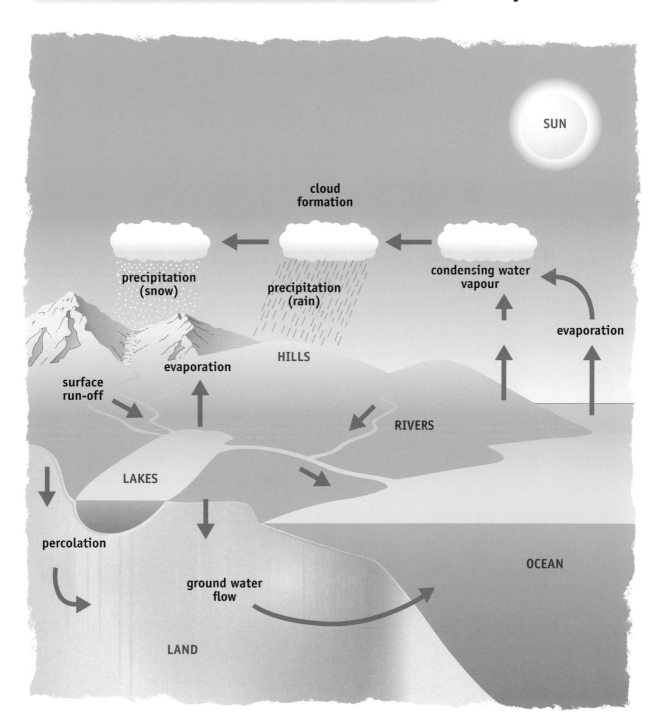

SUN

cloud
formation

precipitation
(snow)

precipitation
(rain)

condensing water
vapour

evaporation

HILLS

evaporation

surface
run-off

RIVERS

LAKES

percolation

OCEAN

ground water
flow

LAND

# Pollution and other problems

▲ Rubbish and poisonous chemicals have been dumped into water, making it unsafe for people and animals.

Water is one of our most valuable natural resources. (A natural resource is a substance found in nature that has many important uses.) Unfortunately, not all water is safe to use. Water can carry **germs** and diseases. It can be **polluted** by poisonous **chemicals**, rubbish, and waste.

Water picks up anything it comes into contact with, including dirt, grease, and grime. It picks up soap, bleach, and other cleaning products. It carries with it **pesticides** and **fertilizers** used on plants. All these things make the water unsafe. It has to be cleaned and **filtered** at a **water treatment facility** before it can be used.

**The Gulf oil spill**

On 20 April 2010, an explosion on an oil rig caused nearly 5 million barrels of oil to come spilling out of an underwater oil well in the Gulf of Mexico. (A barrel is about 160 litres.) Eleven workers died. Fish, birds, and other marine wildlife suffered great harm. So did the families that live along the Gulf. They depend on fishing, shipping, oil production, and tourism for their income. It took more than 100 days to seal the well and clean up the mess.

◀ Water pollution is a problem for wildlife as well as for people.

▲ During a drought, communities limit the amount of water people are allowed to use and ask them to save as much water as possible.

## The problem of drought

A drought is a long season of dry weather that causes water supplies to run low – or run out. Without water, farmers lose their crops and their animals suffer. Food shortages can occur.

> ### Water in Africa
>
> In Africa, people don't have as much access to clean water. The average person uses only 38 litres (10 gallons) a day. In some villages, girls and women spend as much as three hours a day travelling back and forth to the nearest water supply to collect water for their families.

# The problem of waste

In the United Kingdom, an average person uses 150 litres (33 gallons) of water each day. Many people use about 9 litres (2 gallons) of water just to brush their teeth! It takes 6–27 litres (1.3–6 gallons) to flush a toilet and 34–45 litres (7–10 gallons) to run a dishwasher – 76 litres (17 gallons) if you wash the dishes in the sink. A bath can take up to 80 litres (18 gallons) of water. Too often, water is wasted. We could all use a lot less.

**Animals**

Desert animals have found special ways to get the water they need. The fat in camels' humps changes into water as it breaks down. Gerbils and **kangaroo rats** get water from the plants they eat. Snakes and lizards collect moisture from the morning dew. They lick the tiny droplets that form on their own bodies!

▼ Turning the water off while you brush is a great way to save water.

23

# Saving water

 **If we each do our part, there will be plenty of water for everyone.**

## Water source ✓

In the United Kingdom, only one per cent of people have to rely on wells for water. Everyone else receives their water through public water facilities.

We can all help preserve our water supply. We can turn off taps and hosepipes when we're not using them. We can use less water in the bath or take quick showers instead. Fixing leaky pipes saves water, too.

## Cleaning water

Scientists are always looking for better ways to clean and reuse our fresh water. **Water treatment facilities recycle** water. They **filter** out rubbish. They remove dirt, **bacteria**, **viruses**, **parasites**, and **chemicals**. Laws have been passed that require chemical companies and factories to dispose of their waste in a way that won't hurt the environment.

## Five more ways to save

1. Use a watering can instead of a hosepipe or sprinklers to water your garden.

2. Run your dishwasher or washing machine only when they are full. You'll save 3,785 litres (833 gallons) of water a month.

3. Reuse your towels several times before putting them in the washing basket. In between uses, hang them up to dry.

4. When you give your pet fresh water, don't dump the old water down the drain. Use it to water your plants.

5. Share what you've learned about saving water with your friends and family.

▼ Water is cleaned and recycled at water treatment facilities like this one.

# Water for the world

▲ These people in Senegal are getting water from a well.

In the last 20 years, more than a billion people all over the world have been given access to fresh, clean water for the first time. More than a billion still don't have safe water.

Community groups and organizations such as the **United Nations** are working together to change this.

## Aquifers

In most places, water can be found under ground. There are underground streams and springs. Water also collects in little pockets or pools between layers of rocky soil. These are called aquifers. Digging or drilling in the soil releases the water and brings it to the surface, where people can use it.

These groups teach people not to **pollute** their own water supply. They teach them how to conserve (save) the fresh water they have. They help them dig wells, so that the people don't have to drink from rivers or streams full of wastewater. Meanwhile, scientists are searching for new and inexpensive ways to **filter** and clean polluted water.

## World Water Day

On 22 March 1993, the United Nations created International World Water Day. It is a day to remember how much we all need pure, clean water, and how important it is to use our water wisely. It is also a day for countries to come together to talk about their water problems and help each other find solutions.

▼ Working together, we can make sure there is water for everyone!

# Timeline

(These dates are often approximations.)

**3000 BC**
The ancient Egyptians build their **civilization** on the River Nile.

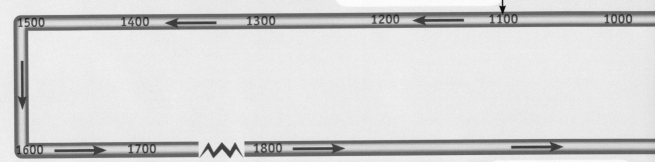

3000 BC

**AD 1100–1400**
During the Middle Ages, waterwheels are used to power the first factories and machines.

| 1500 | 1400 | 1300 | 1200 | 1100 | 1000 |

1600 — 1700 — 1800 —

**1882**
The first hydroelectric power plant begins operating in Wisconsin, USA.

**1993**
The **United Nations** announces the first International World Water Day – 22 March.

1900

**2008**
The Three Gorges Dam in China becomes the largest in the world, producing more than 15 times the hydroelectric power of the Hoover Dam.

**2009**
NASA announces that it has found small amounts of water on the Moon.

2000

This symbol shows where there is a change of scale in the timeline, or where a long period of time with no noted events has been left out.

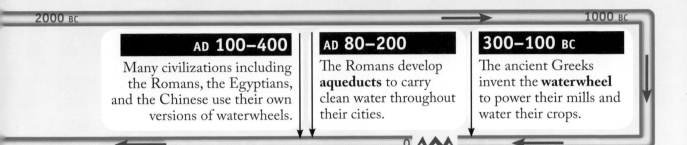

**2000 BC** ━━━━━━━━━━━━━━━━━━━━━━━→ **1000 BC**

### AD 100–400
Many civilizations including the Romans, the Egyptians, and the Chinese use their own versions of waterwheels.

### AD 80–200
The Romans develop **aqueducts** to carry clean water throughout their cities.

### 300–100 BC
The ancient Greeks invent the **waterwheel** to power their mills and water their crops.

0

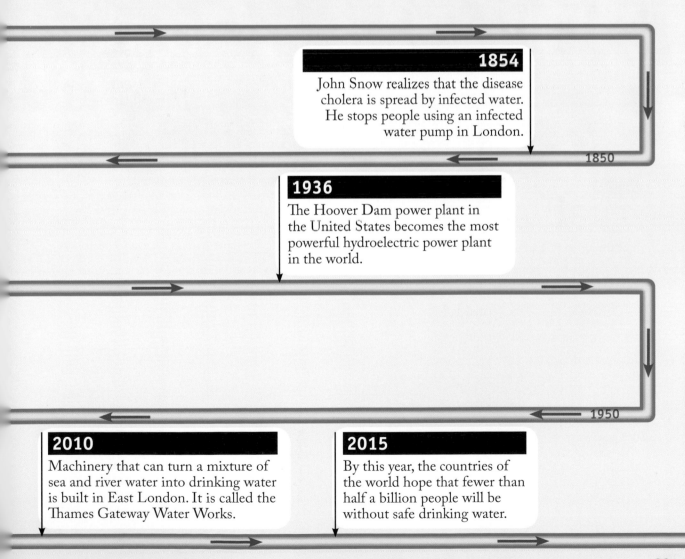

### 1854
John Snow realizes that the disease cholera is spread by infected water. He stops people using an infected water pump in London.

**1850**

### 1936
The Hoover Dam power plant in the United States becomes the most powerful hydroelectric power plant in the world.

**1950**

### 2010
Machinery that can turn a mixture of sea and river water into drinking water is built in East London. It is called the Thames Gateway Water Works.

### 2015
By this year, the countries of the world hope that fewer than half a billion people will be without safe drinking water.

# Glossary

**aqueduct** system of bridges and tunnels that carries clean water throughout a city

**atom** tiniest part of an element, a substance that cannot be made any smaller

**bacteria** tiny living things which can only be seen using a microscope

**bog** very soft, wet area of land with layers of plant material on it

**chemical** substance that can be made into other substances by changing its atoms or molecules

**civilization** culture of a particular time or place

**evaporate** change from a liquid into a gas or vapour

**fertilizer** substance that helps plants grow

**filter** allow water to go through a device to separate unwanted matter from it

**gas** air-like substance that will spread to fill any space around it

**germ** tiny living or non-living thing that enters the body and can cause diseases

**glacier** large body of ice that moves slowly down a slope or valley

**kangaroo rat** rodent that lives in the deserts of North America and travels by hopping on its long hind legs

**hail** lump of hard snow and ice

**hydroelectricity** electricity made from the energy produced by running water

**liquid** material that takes up a definite amount of space but has no shape of its own

**marsh** wet, grassy area of land

**mineral** substance that is naturally present in the earth, such as salt and gold

**molecule** tiny particle composed of one or more atoms

**parasite** tiny plant or animal that lives on or inside another plant or animal

**pesticide** chemical used to kill harmful insects and other pests

**polar ice cap** ice and snow that cover the North and South poles

**pollute** cause harmful materials to destroy Earth's natural resources

**pollution** harmful materials that destroy Earth's natural resources

**recycle** use over again – sometimes in a new way

**solid** any substance that is hard and firm and has its own shape

**solvent** substance that makes other substances dissolve or break down

**swamp** area of land that is very wet and may be covered with water, where there are woody plants and trees

**tide** rising and falling of the surface of oceans

**United Nations** international organization that works to increase co-operation between countries to promote peace and the well-being of people around the world

**virus** tiny thing that grows and multiplies within other, living things, causing an infectious disease

**waterwheel** large wheel that is turned by water flowing over or under it

**water treatment facility** factory where wastewater is cleaned so that it can be reused

**water vapour** gas that water changes into when it is heated

# Find out more

## Books

*Water* (Go Facts: Environmental Issues), Blakes (A & C Black, 2007)

*Water* (What Happens When We Recycle), Jillian Powell (Franklin Watts, 2008)

*The Water Cycle* (Earth's Processes), Rebecca Harman (Heinemann Library, 2005)

*Water for Everyone* (Headline Issues), Sarah Levete (Heinemann Library, 2009)

*Water Wise*, Alison Hawes (A & C Black, 2010)

## Websites

**www.metoffice.gov.uk/education/teachers/popup/popup_wboardap_
water_cycle.html**
Watch an animation of the water cycle on this web page.

**apps.sepa.org.uk/floodlinekids/index.html**
Learn more about water on this site.

## Places to visit

Thames Barrier Information and Learning Centre
1 Unity Way
Woolwich
London SE18 5NJ
Telephone: 020 8305 4188
**www.greenwich.gov.uk/Greenwich/LeisureCulture/MuseumsAndGalleries/
ThamesBarrierLearningCentre**
Learn about the history and environment of the River Thames and find out how the Thames Barrier was designed and built and how it works.

Scottish Hydro Electric Visitor Centre
Pitlochry
Perthshire PH16 5ND
Telephone: 01796 473152
**www.scottish-southern.co.uk/SSEInternet/index.aspx?id=538**
Trace the history of hydrogeneration in Scotland from its origins in the 1940s to the present.

# Index